Holding
Heaven and Earth
in One Hand

Holding Heaven and Earth in One Hand

A True Story about Living and Dying

NANCY COBBLE, M.D.
WITH
JOY SAWYER

Judson Press ® Valley Forge

Holding Heaven and Earth in One Hand:
A True Story about Living and Dying
© 1998 by Judson Press, Valley Forge, PA 19482-0851
All rights reserved.

Bible quotations in this volume are from HOLY BIBLE: New International Version, copyright © 1973, 1978, 1984. Used by permission of Zondervan Bible Publishers.

Section sixteen was originally titled "Two Hats" and is reprinted with permission from *Mars Hill Review.* © 1996 *Mars Hill Review.* All rights reserved.

Library of Congress Cataloging-in-Publication Data

Cobble, Nancy.
    Holding heaven and earth in one hand : a true story about living and dying / Nancy Cobble with Joy Sawyer.
        p.   cm.
    ISBN 0-8170-1283-4 (pbk. : alk. paper)
    1. Cobble, Nancy.   2. Christian biography–United States.   3. Physicians–United States–Biography.   4. Cancer–Patients–Religious life.   5. Cancer–Religious aspects–Christianity.   6. Death–Religious aspects–Christianity.   I. Sawyer, Joy.   II. Title.
BR1725.C535A3   1998
248.6'6092–dc21
[B]   98-3334

Printed in the U.S.A.

06 05 04 03 02 01 00 99 98

10 9 8 7 6 5 4 3 2 1

ᴄᴘᴏ Contents ᴄᴘᴏ

❧ *To the Reader* ❧

WHEN JUDSON EDITOR Randy Frame first suggested I write an explanation of how this book developed, my immediate thought was, "What an incredible honor." That's because helping Nancy Cobble write this book — both before her death and after — was nothing less than a glorious, life-changing privilege, from beginning to end. I feel most fortunate that I was allowed the pleasure of knowing and loving this remarkable woman, who, over the course of time, also became my very dear friend.

I was first introduced to Nancy by a counselor friend, Al Andrews, who at the time was Nancy's therapist. "I want you to meet an amazing woman," he told me. He then explained that a few years prior Nancy had been diagnosed with terminal cancer — and, quite miraculously, had gone into a several-year remission. In the time she had remaining, Al explained, this woman wanted to learn how to love her family and friends better. "Nancy's learning how to live with her 'bags unpacked,' as she calls it," he told me, "and wants to write a book about her journey. Will you help her?"

Upon meeting Nancy, I was immediately struck by, of all things, her hair. After enduring several grueling rounds of chemotherapy, Nancy had exchanged her bald head for a gorgeous, shiny, chin-length, auburn wig. I soon realized this woman's playful hairstyle suited perfectly the lively, bubbling woman within. She showed me a short piece she'd written, which she'd entitled, "This Story."

"Everyone has a story," she told me, "but I wanted to tell *this* story among many." After I read the contents of this woman's heart on paper, I wept. I knew that working on this project with her would not simply be a one-way street; there was no way I would walk away from this woman's story — and her soul — unchanged.

I encouraged Nancy to journal as much as she could, while I worked on editing her work. In the meantime, Nancy set out to live life to its fullest. She painted. She joined a women's support group I was co-leading at the time. She also transcribed, word for word, all of the counseling sessions she'd had with Al Andrews — a painstaking feat. She didn't know if she wanted them in the book, she told me, but typing the words on paper helped her to relive and re-experience the meaningful times she'd shared with Al, whom she deeply respected and loved.

At the time, my husband, Scott, was the editor of a literary journal called the *Mars Hill Review*. Together, he and I edited a short piece of Nancy's writing, "Two Hats," for publication in the Spring 1996 issue of *MHR*. When Nancy told us in late January 1996 that her cancer had returned, she was able to see the galleys of that piece in print — and was thoroughly delighted. "I've never wanted to be *just* a doctor," she laughed. "I've wanted to be an artist, too." We rejoiced together that her dream had finally come true.

When Nancy realized she was dying, she had a request for me — she wanted me to write a poem for her funeral. I agreed, but told her I wanted her to hear it before she left us for good. One Friday, I finished the poem and called the house to read it to her. Ron, her husband, told me she wasn't feeling well, but that she'd call me back as soon as she was up and around. Two days later, on Sunday, March 17, 1996, Nancy packed her bags for the last time and journeyed home to her Father in heaven. She first heard my words of tribute at her own memorial service.*

Nancy requested that I have full access to all her journals and papers in order to select what was to be included in the book. She also asked me to shape and rewrite her words so that they'd read clearly and smoothly. "Make it poetic," she giggled. "Not medical doctor-ish." I worked on the book for over a year, and I'd often hear her voice in my mind as I made various editorial choices on what,

---

*Editor's note: Joy's poem, "The Woman with Wings," can be found on page 113.

or what not, to include. I knew Nancy well enough to know she'd want her words to heal and not to hurt — yet I also know she'd want the book to be as honest and straightforward as possible.

Nancy Cobble's earnest hope, and mine as well, is that this story, her story, could somehow connect with each of our stories. May we discover anew what it means to live and love fully, by holding the wonders of heaven and the struggles of earth together, in one hand.

JOY SAWYER

∽ Foreword ∽

Nancy Cobble was my wife, and this is her story—a healing story, a holy story, a story I lived alongside her. *Holding Heaven and Earth in One Hand* is the story of her journey of faith amidst the devastation of cancer.

Over the course of nearly two years, Nancy faithfully picked up her pen and wrote down her experiences. Hers was a very peculiar journey, because she wore two very different hats: both a doctor's and a cancer patient's. Yet, remarkably, Nancy wore them both with style, grace, and dignity—coupled with an honest, searching faith.

Early on during our journey through this dark, mysterious valley, Nancy and I determined we'd be open, honest, and revealing to all those who asked us the question, "How are things going?" Yet the surprising thing about Nancy's voyage through suffering is that, perhaps for the first time in her life, I watched her develop a deep trust in her God—a trust despite her fear. She experienced joy in the journey, despite all the chaos that raged around her. She learned to hear God speaking to her, "Do not fear, for I am with you," in the midst of terrifying circumstances. Her trust in her Lord touched all those near her. I pray that as you read her words that you will experience that same trust.

Nancy and I seldom asked the question, "Why?" Rather, we learned to ask, "What now? How do you want to work in my life, God? How do you want to use me? How do I learn to pursue life passionately, to 'live well' for as long as I can?"

I read recently that people with scuff marks make the best companions. Nancy Cobble was a woman with scuff marks, and I can tell you she was an incredible companion. In these words she's written, she welcomes you to watch and learn as she walks her path of suffering.

RON COBBLE

March 1997

✑ *Introduction* ✑

I WOULD LIKE TO TELL YOU why I'm writing this book. I'm a woman physician, a wife of fifteen years, a mom of ten years, and a Christian. As I write these words, it's been over two years since I was diagnosed with terminal cancer and, to my surprise, I am still here. I've lived way beyond what anyone expected. Somewhere along the way, I crossed back over the invisible line that divides dying from living, and I am grateful for the time I still have left.

But I'm finding that my path leading to the "land of the living" isn't straightforward, isn't without some strange twists and turns. I've found that it's difficult to prepare to die, and then to have to live again. You see, after my diagnosis, I packed my bags, so to speak, and simply prepared for my trip home. My plan was simple: to carry my suitcases and to keep walking, step by step, through the territory that belonged to death.

As you might imagine, I found death a difficult companion. As I traveled, death dogged my every step, gloating over the fact that, as a human, I belonged to him. The only way I could keep moving forward was to walk with my face turned away from him and pointed toward my God's, holding His hand tightly, seeing the love and joy mirrored in His eyes. But that wasn't the hardest part of my journey. Nothing prepared me for the surprising detour I encountered: having to leave my companion, death, behind — and returning to a life of *life*.

For now, I've discovered I can put my suitcases down, but I must still leave them packed. My journey home may resume at any minute. Now it is more complicated: I have more questions, more sorrow, more indecisiveness. I'm feeling different things inside, and I've realized that, maybe, I am far enough away from the horror of my disease that it's safe for me to look it in the eye — and to truly feel what I need to feel, in order to write these words.

So why am I telling this story?

First, for myself . . .

I want to feel and declare what is most important and most real to me . . . because this story is my story. I want to live life to the fullest during the time I have left and, hopefully, to discover God trustworthy in all of it.

For my family, especially Chris and Dan, my two boys . . .

To leave those I love a connection with me and with the Lord whom I serve, and to give them a written account of my hopes and beliefs in and for them.

For others . . .

To offer the gifts of what God has shown me (so

far) about living, dying, and moving forward into the unknown — and into the shelter of the Lord.

For Cherri Parks...

Who started this process by living through her own sister's death — and who first invited me to tell this story.

March 1994

Part I

A Journey to the Edge

✑ *One* ✑

MY JOURNEY toward the edge of dying began in March 1992 — the no-man's-land time between winter and spring. As a doctor, I pay close attention to physical details, so I began to worry when I experienced some strange symptoms: it hurt to breathe — right in the middle of my abdomen — and I was running a low-grade fever. After a couple of days both the fever and pain went away, and to say I was relieved is an understatement. I wanted to ignore it — something that, throughout my life, I'd learned to do quite well. One of the cardinal rules I'd lived by was: "If something disappears, you don't have to deal with it." Besides, my husband, Ron, was preparing to take a trip with our two boys, Chris and Dan, to watch baseball spring training — and I didn't want anything to interfere with *that*.

During the next month, even though I remained pain-free, I could tell that something still was not right. I had a weird, hollow feeling inside, which by April had progressed into profound fatigue. Must be the flu, I thought. I also was working for two medical programs at the time, and one of them required a fifty-mile commute.

Then suddenly the pain came back: with each deep breath, a startling pain hit me, right below my rib cage. And with it came a triple-nasty trigger point between my neck and shoulder (which I later discovered was "referred pain" from what was happening internally). A few days later, after spending a night of groaning and tossing back and forth in pain, I called a doctor colleague of mine, Dr. K. She cleared her schedule to see me just a few hours after my call.

Dr. K. was puzzled by my symptoms. Obviously, I was in great agony, because I could barely move. I felt like someone was gripping, twisting, and wrenching my insides — and kicking me in the gut at the same time. The doctor screened my heart and lungs, took x-rays and did blood work, and gave me some pain medication — which promptly made me sicker.

The next day I was back wearing my "physician's hat" when Dr. K. called me with a slight problem: the tests showed my liver was enlarged and that the liver-related blood tests were abnormal. She tried very hard to be neutral, mentioning it was "probably something like hepatitis." As doctors, we both knew "something like hepatitis" would be a good explanation for my being so sick, and that it would be nicely treatable: bed rest and broth. She suggested I come in for more tests. I said to myself, Don't panic. Wait and see. There's no use wasting energy panicking now.

I showed up the next day for an ultrasound of my liver. After the technician took her pictures, she then told me she was going to call the radiologist. To get the opinion of this particular doctor, she told me, was a very common thing and nothing to worry about. Yet, as a doctor, I knew enough to suspect that "calling the radiologist" was not all that common.

The doctor came into my room and studied the images. The viewing screen had been turned away from me, and I saw him staring silently at the pictures. I asked him to shoot me straight about what he saw. "Metastatic cancer throughout your liver," he said. Poor guy. He didn't even know me — and I made *him* be the one to give me the news first. I don't even remember what he looked like.

Then I was climbing off the exam table, getting dressed, walking back to my own doctor's office in the next building. Was this a new thing in my life? Was I a new person? Was this a new universe I'd stumbled into? I carefully repeated the words over and over to my-self, trying to make them real: Cancer, cancer? cancer! CANCER, all the different inflections and nuances you can hear in one word.

Oh, God! Cancer.

Dr. K. met me at her office during lunch hour. I called Ron at work. Would he be where I could find him? He was often away during lunch, but I needed him now.

Thank God, he answered the phone. I told him simply that the doctors had discovered something serious, and I needed him to be with me. He immediately came to the doctor's office.

As Ron and I held hands, Dr. K. gently reviewed the diagnosis with us. "This is cancer," she said, "and what is in your liver has obviously spread from somewhere else. The pain you're experiencing is due to your liver being stretched by the cancer's rapid growth." She arranged for a referral to a cancer specialist, someone I knew and liked, someone I had worked with myself when I was the physician discovering unknown cancer in *my* patient. My doctor desperately wanted to give me something, anything. She offered me pills to help me sleep, pills to help me remain calm — even a little bottle of airplane whiskey (which I've kept). She offered us what she could, and we were grateful.

I only cried a little that day in her office. I could feel myself not wanting to face the difficult times coming, but I also knew that all the answers weren't in yet. It looked bad, but there were still a fairly significant number of possibilities; we just needed to explore them.

Ron took the rest of the day off. We ate lunch outside; it tasted so good. I immediately experienced a strange sense of gratitude in the moment for every good thing. In a way it didn't make sense — my world had changed irrevocably. But there was a sweetness, an aliveness, to that particular lunch with Ron on that spring day.

Later that evening, I called my best friend, Dottie, my friend throughout almost all the years I'd lived in Denver. She cried for me, and she hated my news. She was furious with the disease and angrily declared that "this shouldn't be!" I recognized her feelings and appreciated her love for me, but I didn't feel those feelings for myself.

At least, not yet.

✎ *Two* ✎

THE VERY FIRST QUESTION I asked upon learning I had cancer was, "Does this disastrous circumstance now prove that God doesn't exist? Or, worse — that He exists, but is either weak or untrustworthy, or both?" This was a particularly tricky question for me, since I'd always struggled with the meaning of evil and suffering in other people's lives. Didn't all that pain somehow negate the existence of a good God? I remembered having argued with God, "Why not make it clear that good follows Your children? Then more people will seek You."

Now that evil had wormed its way into my own life, my first rock-bottom question was, "Do I really trust Him?"

Somehow, I'm sure by the very grace of God I did trust Him. Perhaps I knew it would be too awful and impossible to even consider thinking God wasn't real; I don't know. But I found that my trust was occurring in new ways, in moment-by-moment real ways. It's almost as if I felt Him asking me: "Do you trust Me with this illness, to work it out for the best? Do you trust Me for

My goodness in this? Do you trust Me for My power to be displayed in this?" (Well, there went demanding a cure!) "Do you trust Me enough to give up your right to be healthy?" (There went holding on to bitterness.) "Do you trust Me for your family's welfare?" (But it will hurt so much, God. How can all of this be right?) "Do you trust Me even if you can't see anything ahead of you?"

Yes.

Miraculously, I learned to receive from Him the life I was now living with trust and, strangely, joy — while at the same time not ever attributing the cause of the sickness to Him. Because of that trust, I said, "I take Your hand, and look to You, and rest in what You are doing." Once the question of trust was answered, the question of "Why me?" never came up. It became irrelevant, beside the point. Even if the question could have been answered, I know now the answer wouldn't have been important. Instead, the question I found myself asking was clearly, "What now, Lord?"

∽ *Three* ∽

I WENT BACK TO THE HOSPITAL for a liver biopsy — to find out exactly what kind of cancer this was. The general appearance of the cancer cells under the microscope could tell us more about the source of the disease, the possibility of treatment, and the expected outcome. It was during this time that I discovered just what it feels like to be a patient rather than a doctor.

As the dye was injected for my CT scan, the technician remarked that, if the stuff happened to leak, it would be unbearably painful. The radiologist handling the large biopsy needle remarked that this type of liver biopsy was usually excruciating. So I asked him for pain medication far in advance. Why wait to hurt? But strangely, I never did. I still don't understand why.

After the biopsy, I went to the day-surgery recovery area to stabilize and to wait for the preliminary diagnosis: the pathologist's initial impressions of the cancer. While I was waiting, I called a friend, a former co-worker there at the hospital, who had once been my advocate during a difficult work situation.

He came and put his hand on my shoulder. As I told him what I was going through, I felt him shaking. Then it dawned on me: he was crying over my story — the story I'd found difficult to grieve over yet. Yet his anguish felt like more than just his own sorrow for me. In a way, it felt as if he were shedding the tears I had not yet shed. Once again, I felt profound gratitude over this very small, intimate provision.

The preliminary diagnosis was confusing: "It appears there are some neural fibers. Perhaps it is a neuro-endocrine tumor." I'd never heard of this malady before, and I couldn't understand what was implied by the diagnosis. But whatever it was, it appeared to encourage the pathologist and oncologist. It was possible that this tumor had spread quickly and extensively throughout the liver, but then had never gone any further.

I lived with this hope for several days, but the next report that came wasn't as promising. I had the diagnosis evaluated by two other experts, but the answer was always the same: "What you have is not the kind of tumor that stays in one place. It is primitive, wild, uncontrolled, not just a little malignant, but *very* malignant."

And, I thought to myself, *very malevolent*.

The next step was to undergo a series of medical tests to try and locate the cancer's source and to find evidence of its spread. Ron went with me for the first test, but mostly I went to these appointments alone. These sessions involved a lot of waiting, and undressing, and lots of cold rooms and holding still, and much poking and prodding. I was determined I could face this trauma myself; I thought I could handle it myself. The overwhelming need to have someone close would hit me later.

The first tests were negative: no source or spread seen in a bone scan, two mammograms, and an upper GI. Finally, during a barium enema (truly one of the most uncomfortable and grossest tests ever devised), they found the source: a golf ball-sized mass in my large intestine. It had been a secret; no symptoms, no signs. As a physician, I was grateful it wasn't my fault I'd missed finding it.

Now that we'd discovered the source, the visible extent, and the basic nature of the cancer, we needed to set a course of treatment. The following week, I met with a surgeon, who recommended that we cut out the mass. At the time, I wondered why we waited a whole week before we decided what to do. It's only in retrospect I understand: the doctors knew it was already too late for a cure; ultimately, nothing could be done to save my life — so another week truly did not matter.

The surgeon carefully explained to me that, not only should we remove the primary cancer, but that if I were to have chemotherapy to try to dissolve the rest, I would be left with a hole in my gut where the malignancy was. That, in turn, would leak all over my insides and kill me.

So I planned for surgery the following week.

Only once during those first few days did I "lose it." I was the medical director for a brain injury rehabilitation program, and as soon as I knew the news, I told my team I had cancer. But I told my nurse assistant even more — that my liver was full of the disease. We both knew that couldn't be good. I left work early, feeling a little crazy and sad. I could talk about it, but it just didn't feel real to me, not yet.

✐ *Four* ✐

I WAS NOW feeling sicker by the day. I slowly started to phone the important people in my life to tell them the news — and to find out what was happening in their lives. I felt I needed to say to them, "You are an important person in my life. I need to tell you about me." Ordinarily, I wouldn't have shared this sort of thing aloud, but something had changed in me. It felt good to do so, strangely, even a *joy* to do so.

And I kept working. I continued working as the doctor until it was time for me to switch hats and to become the patient. I was so exhausted that, every few minutes, I would sit on the floor with my head on a chair. I also kept playing my tympani with the church orchestra, preparing for the Easter service. I loved the music, and I thought it would be the last time I could make music with others for God.

The idea of food was okay, but I couldn't eat. There was no room for food in my stomach. I was constantly thirsty, but could only muster small sips of water. The pain pills made me ill, too, and besides that, they weren't working. I hurt. Four days before surgery was scheduled, I called the doctor. How am I going to make it through surgery when I feel so bad? I asked. Thankfully, she arranged for me to come into the hospital the next day, Easter Sunday. Sadly, instead of playing my tympani, I watched the Easter program from the audience.

Ron and I and the boys went out to breakfast after church. We'd told the boys I was very sick, that I had cancer, and that I'd be heading into the hospital for treatment. Chris and Dan (ages eight and four then) barely responded. We couldn't tell if they'd understood us. Then, very carefully (and trying hard to be casual), Chris asked if I was going to die. I said I didn't know, but that I'd do everything I possibly could to get better, and that I didn't want to leave them.

Then I went to the hospital.

When I finally got to my room, I started vomiting. My liver was so full of cancer it wouldn't work anymore. I slept for hours, and, ironically, I found myself truly grateful to be in the hospital, where I could be cared for. The first few days were tolerable: lots of needles, more tests hunting for hidden cancer, but, on the whole, not too bad — until the morning of surgery. I woke up so scared I thought I'd throw up from just being afraid — and I carried the wash pan with me as they wheeled me down to the pre-op area.

∽

Very early on, just a few days after my world was unmade by my diagnosis, I heard a thought in the middle of the night: "Do not fear, for I am with you." It seemed so simple, but those words became the centerpiece of the table on which I would dine daily.

The directive "Do not fear" was a direct quote from God, in Isaiah 41:10. The response is from Psalm 23: "Even though I walk through the valley of the shadow of death, I will fear no evil, for You are with me." That is what I am to do, I thought. I am in death's territory, in his valley, and he is walking with me. But I do not fear evil, for my Lord is right beside me.

I grieved, because I didn't know if I would handle well everything heading my way. I was anxious, and terrified sometimes. There was lots to be afraid of: growing sicker, becoming physically repulsive, pain, procedures, separation, leaving home for the last time, all the possible ways of dying from this disease (as many different ways as there are different organs). All those things were true. Yet, at the same time, I learned to not fear.

I learned in the midst of my struggle that the "do not fear" part can't be created or manufactured or chosen. I learned I couldn't even ask God to "give it" to me, as if not fearing were a gift. The not fearing was His being with me, and my attention directed at Him. When I kept looking to Him, being with Him, then He was between me and my fear, and I was at rest.

✍ *Five* ✍

AFTER SURGERY, I was the patient again, not the doctor. I was hooked up to three or four different IV lines all the time, each IV pump beeping with a different tone and rate. I didn't know what all the beeps were, but I often heard a new one in the middle of the night. And, even though I was on self-administered IV narcotic pain medication, I was still in tremendous pain. In fact, I could barely move — and rolling over became a nearly impossible struggle. My elbows were rubbed raw from pushing against my sheets as I frantically tried to get some leverage. All the patients I had ever cared for as a doctor, all the people who had desperately sought me for medical help and who had struggled with their own weakness, suddenly became more real to me.

It was lonely at night, and I cried.

The doctors told me what they'd found during surgery: the cancer had already spread through the intestine wall, past some local lymph nodes, as well as into the liver.

Clearly, it hadn't been contained. They'd removed the section of large intestine around the cancer and then sewed the rest of the intestine back together — but they couldn't do a thing with my liver. The cancer was spread throughout. All they could do was biopsy another large piece to make a still more accurate diagnosis and also prognosis. The final results, they told me, would take a few more days.

There were two conversations during those early days of my illness that stuck with me. Each of those conversations spoke to me concerning what it meant to live — and possibly die — with this illness. The first was a visit with a co-worker. We'd done some good work together in caring for our patients, and I genuinely liked her. She said, "It's obvious you have such great faith. I wish I had faith like that — it's getting you through this." I appreciated her admiration, but I knew in my heart I couldn't accept what she said. The truth was that it wasn't at all my great faith that was getting me through — but the Great Person whom I had faith in and a relationship with. He was the one I was counting on and relying upon, not my faith. There seemed to be a difference in my mind.

The other encounter was with a young doctor, a remote acquaintance, who came to visit me. He flung himself down on the hospital room couch in his usual joking manner, but it was clear he was there for more than just a friendly visit. During our time, he shared with me that he, too, had crossed into the world I had so recently entered. He had cancer, although no one else at work knew it, and he told me it was "the pits."

He laughed as he told me this, but it was an angry, despairing, bitter laugh. Even though I was touched by his willingness to be vulnerable, I was chilled by my sense of his living in an enormous, black hole — living bravely, yet still in total darkness. He did not have Someone to trust with his pain. He brought me flowers — purple chrysanthemums — and told me stories of his childhood. He was doing what he could for me, but I was struck by the sadness that he was doing it all alone. He had no source to turn to except himself.

Then something dawned on me: the grace bestowed upon me was that, in that moment, I knew instantly and profoundly that I could *never* do it alone. My Lord, Jesus Christ, stood between me and my illness. He stood between me and the hideous. Without Him, life — and death — would be sheer madness, a series of impossible escape attempts from impossible horror. Instead, underneath the shelter of His wings, I was experiencing health and wholeness as a person, apart from my physical body. I had hope.

~ *Six* ~

A FEW DAYS after surgery, Ron arrived at my hospital room, just as the doctor entered to give me the final diagnosis. She had been detained until just the time when Ron could be there, and it felt like a special gift from God. The final report (i.e., no more possibilities — all the information was now present and accounted for) was not good. I had a very primitive and probably uncontrollable type of cancer. In fact, this particular form of cancer was extremely rare, she told us. Only twelve other cases had ever been documented.

We asked her to shoot us straight: what is the prognosis? Her reply was also straight: if the chemotherapy works at all, life expectancy is one to five years. There is no cure, she said. The available treatment will never be able to kill off every cancer cell.

Then she left.

No sooner than she'd gone, our pastor walked in. We told him what we'd just heard, and his response to us was wonderful — that is, full of wonder. No platitudes, no diversions from the real issue, not even any heart-felt appeals for healing. We were there together, sitting in a kind of "oh, wow!..." feeling. We all realized I was probably just beginning a common journey, one they would someday take as well — and the sheer wonder of that fact weighed heavily upon our hearts.

My doctor began talking about chemotherapy. I needed to begin the treatment soon, but not too soon. Once chemo began, normal tissue would stop repairing itself at a normal rate. That meant if the surgical incisions had not healed enough by the time chemo started, they would simply fall apart.

Finally, there was simply no choice: I awoke early one morning with a not-a-surgery kind of pain, bad pain, and called the nurse in tears, terrified something was wrong. It was the cancer growing again, stretching and killing off more of my liver. Ready or not, we had to start chemotherapy: cisplatin and VP-16, along with medicine to keep me from vomiting.

I hated chemo. I knew I had to receive it into my body, give it permission to work, but I also hated it. I realized the concept was to see how many cancer cells could die without killing too much of me with them. It was pure liquid poison. The stuff even looked like poison: the bag hanging over my bed and hooked into my IV line had a strange, shiny quality — clear and oily, but menacing, not at all beautiful.

The first time I had chemotherapy I was so anxious I could barely keep from crying. Even antianxiety medication didn't help. Its immediate effect was that it made me both sick and smell bad. Later on, it would make me ugly. Yet that was the price I'd pay to stay alive, however long that would be. I knew this procedure would continue the rest of my life.

Ironically, in the very midst of the absence of health, I found great joy in praising God as the Healer. And, even more ironic, that joy existed apart from any expectation of what God would choose to do as the Healer in my own situation. The joy stemmed from a very sure and certain awareness that, in this universe somewhere, there exists a vast, good God, the Healer. God: health. It was a strange and wonderful comfort.

✑ Seven ✑

ACH TIME I underwent chemotherapy, I read a children's story, one of the *Chronicles of Narnia* by C. S. Lewis, and traveled to good places in my heart. Somehow, the "goodness" of the stories counteracted the "badness" of the chemotherapy and allowed me to receive it. Some other things balanced out the poison and the invasions I was experiencing — things outside my body. My room was filled with flowers, a whole wall full of them, sitting on shelves, on counters, on tables. It was wonderful. They smelled so good. They looked so pretty.

Those flowers spoke to me of people pulling for me, praying for me, wanting me to get better. They made a difference. I never imagined something like receiving flowers, which I once thought of as frivolous and wasteful, could actually feel so good. Someone was even wise enough to give me a big tub of jelly beans. I couldn't eat any myself, but I always had something to offer those who came to visit me in my hospital room.

People also simply gave the gift of themselves. The physician who'd delivered my babies offered me his home phone number to call anytime, just in case I needed someone to talk to. There were wonderful visits and visitors. A bouncy, upbeat surgeon, a little older than I, came to chat. He revealed that he, too, was fighting cancer. He'd been undergoing chemotherapy for twelve years and had already lived longer than anyone had ever dreamed. Even the nurses from my old rehab unit, where I had been the medical director, dropped in almost daily. Those nurses took me on my first long, outside walk — and they made me laugh. People popped in and told me I looked wonderful. They touched me and gave me hugs. They listened when I talked, and they brought to me precious gifts: the ordinary stories of their lives. There wasn't anything in particular that touched me about these visits; it was just their "being there" that felt important.

I was determined to stay connected with people. I would not be phony, but neither would I be scary. I wanted to be honest about what was happening and what I was feeling, and I wanted to keep reaching out beyond my illness. It felt to me as if there had to be more to my connections with people than just my illness. I desperately wanted to know about their "conversations-at-the-water-cooler," the everyday occurrences in their lives. I wanted to be connected to their ordinariness, their routines. So I purposed I would keep reaching out, letting people know I was comfortable with my obvious condition, and inviting them to journey with me as long as they could. I think now that I didn't want them to leave me behind too soon.

Chris and Dan came to visit almost every day. One evening, as the boys sat on my bed with me, I was able to tell them in depth about what was happening to me. I was so grateful that, even though I was very emotional, I didn't break down. I told them again that the doctors had operated on my cancer, and that the doctors had done everything they could. I told them I was taking some strong, dangerous medicine, but that no one was sure if I would live or not — that my sickness might be bad enough that my body would die. If my body died, I said, then I would live in heaven — but that my preference was to continue to live on earth and be with them. I shared with them that I was sad and scared, but that I was trusting God.

When I finished, the only thing Dan, the youngest, said was that he wanted to see my surgical incision. He looked at the staples remaining in my abdomen and asked if my guts would fall out.

Usually when my boys came to visit me they acted pretty squirrelly. They jumped around, pushed the button that made the hospital bed go up and down, played ball, and retreated into their own world. I think now they didn't know what to do. They were angry and scared and overwhelmed at a world that wasn't behaving according to the rules.

But that night my children were as quiet as they'd ever been while visiting my hospital room. They just sat next to me.

Ron came every day, sometimes twice. We'd sit together on the couch, or on the bed watching TV. The nurses thought we were cute and adorable and they liked it. Occasionally, one of us would cry. Ron said, "But we're such a team — we are such a *good* team. Why would this be taken away from us?" That feels like the most important thing he could have said to me.

Everything became focused on getting me home. I worked hard at being a good patient, even an *exceptionally* good patient: "Yes, of course, you may cut me open and remove my guts. Yes, of course, you may administer poison. Yes, of course, you may ask if I have pooped yet. Yes, of course, you may... and thank you very much." My poor patients, I thought. Truly, I had no idea it was so hard to be on the other end of things. I was being the model patient in my chosen field of rehabilitative medicine, and yet it was still awful.

I even amazed the nursing staff by getting dressed myself — not an easy task with three IV lines still attached. I looked better than I felt. I wanted to go home, but I wasn't able to eat yet — I couldn't even force down the permitted clear liquids. The doctors began intravenous feedings, continuous drips of nasty, yellow-colored fluid. I made jokes about eating steaks and fried potatoes through the IV bags, things I remembered being hungry for once. (The nurses kindly laughed at my comments, even though I suspect they'd heard the joke a hundred times from other patients.)

My insides weren't working yet, so the big deal among my doctors was when and if my bowels would begin functioning again. Every day, several people would ask me about my bowel output — and many useful strategies were used to encourage the same. No one seemed confident they'd get back to normal. I began to get incredibly discouraged: every night I longed more and more for the simple comforts of my home and family, and every morning the surgeon left my room, shaking his head, saying nothing had changed. The hospital had once felt to me like a safety net; now it seemed like a prison.

My escape finally came in the form of Dan's fifth birthday party. I'd arranged — via phone from my hospital room — to throw a big celebration at home, and I informed the doctor there was no way I was going to miss that party. I was leaving the hospital, with or without permission, and furthermore I'd walk home if I had to. So, the doctor granted me a short day pass, even though I was so weak I could barely stand up. Those three party hours left me bone-tired, but I did it: my fifth birthday gift to my son was simply being there.

The next day, my bowels suddenly began functioning again, without warning and without control. It was very messy. I asked the nurse to help me clean up the chair, the floor, the bed, me. "All part of the day's job," she said kindly. All part of nothing working right sooner or later, I said to myself. Just a little taste of the indignity of helplessness to come.

From my journal:

> *In a few days I will have another CT scan. I can hardly stand it this go-round. I don't want to go looking for more cancer. It's almost like it's the fault of the test. If I didn't have to look I wouldn't have to deal with it. But I do have to deal with it. Here it is: this day we have to look it square in the eye. I feel like my life is lived in backward-looking chunks. . . . I find out what it's all about after I've lived it. Now it is time again to see what these last few months of pain were really all about. What is going on inside me? Did the cancer stay quiet? Really, is more cancer growing? Is it time to be a patient again — or do I have to wait?*
>
> *Lately my illness has struck me in new ways. Somehow this knowing now is new: I HAVE CANCER. SOMETHING WENT TERRIBLY WRONG. THIS IS WRONG! But I also continue to feel grateful for each day that has been given to me. This strange sense of gratitude overwhelmed me the very first day I heard the diagnosis — and has stayed. And I find myself grateful to be grateful.*

I read this morning in 2 Corinthians that Paul, when he went to Macedonia, found "conflicts without and fears within." This man who trusted You, God, more than anything, revealed that he found fears within. Isn't that interesting, especially when I'm figuring out what to do with all these feelings that crop up: not only feelings about the illness itself, but about my life and who I am. I think about what I am and haven't been, haven't become, am not, what I've done and haven't done, haven't been able to do, but wished I could dream of doing.

Maybe I am learning that even the "wishing to" is a special part of me, and that if the wishing is mine, so are the fears, regrets, anger, doubts, and all the rest . . . it all is part of who I am — and God is trustworthy with all of it.

∽ *Eight* ∽

I FINALLY did get to go home. The nurse pushed me in a wheelchair — hospital procedure — to the door, where I officially stopped being "the patient." As I approached that doorway, the nurse kissed me — the same nurse who had cleaned me up during my bowel accident. Now she sent me on my way with an embrace. Spring that year was early and warm, and flowers had already opened during those two weeks I was in the hospital. Even though I had missed the flowers budding, I was grateful that all this was happening to me in the spring, while the world was opening up with life. It balanced the evil and death I was fighting inside myself.

Getting home was my only goal then: *my* home, *my* family, right there beside me. Home was good, yes — but I soon discovered it was not the same home I'd left. The end of a central IV line dangled out of my upper chest, which led directly into the entryway of my heart. And I, even though a doctor, absolutely hated needles — yet I had to stab a needle into my own belly every day: an injection to boost production of infection-fighting white blood cells.

I came home a different person — not just because of the fatigue, the nausea, the slowness, the struggle to accomplish the most trivial task, but also because of the vulnerability I felt. I knew that I was mortal. I expected to continue the rest of my life from this place, home, because it seemed only fair: I'd given my all to survive. We all counted on my being home as a sure thing.

Yet five days later, on Mother's Day, we learned that truly, with cancer, there's no such thing as a "sure thing." I was relaxing while Ron was out having fun with the boys. I felt fine. An hour later, I had shaking chills and a soaring fever — and I didn't know where Ron was or when he'd be back. I was furious at him for not being there when I needed him.

I tried to talk the on-call doctor out of my coming back to the hospital immediately, but he was unmoved. I must have looked awful, because our neighbor refused to let me drive myself to the hospital. She dropped everything she was doing and pulled up to my front door — just as Ron arrived home. We didn't say much during that long drive to the emergency room. By midnight, I was lying in a hospital bed with a system-wide infection and practically no white blood cells to fight it off with. My life had journeyed to the edge again. It took another six days and four different antibiotics to pull through.

During that second hospitalization, there were no flowers, few visitors, and my hair fell out — first a few strands, then more and more hair, rapidly and relent-lessly. Chris and Dan dealt with the pain of it by pulling it out for me. I couldn't stand to look in the mirror and see more of my scalp showing.

A few years back, I had a dream in which I realized I had one more chance to grow long, flowing hair — and so I'd grown it. It was an expression of who I was, and now it was gone. Losing my hair was as hard as anything I'd been through. Even though I felt I shouldn't care that much about it, I did. Though losing my hair seemed like nothing compared to losing my life, it still bothered me for a long time. At first, I vowed never to be seen with-out a wig. But even wearing a wig still made me feel shameful, like a prisoner of war, all shaved and branded. I was sorry I had to display my ugliness to others.

Up to this point, I'd accepted all the invasions on my body: the needles, the knives, the poisons. And, as a gift to those fighting for my life, I gave back what I believed to be helpful, calm, pleasant and polite cooper-ation. I also was fiercely determined to have some choice in this awful experience, and cooperating seemed like a choice. Now, one more procedure needed to be done: in order to keep the chemo from killing off my veins, I had to have a port placed permanently under my skin — a small reservoir which could be injected with the chemo-therapy, and which drained directly into the large vessel leading to my heart. I was an outpatient, and I was very much awake when they wheeled me into the cold operating room. And, this time, I was not fully asleep for the painful part, the part when they stretched the skin off the underlying rib cage to make room for the port. I remembered what I was not supposed to remember; and that is when I had second thoughts about "gracefully" receiving treatment. Maybe the next time I'm the patient, I thought, groaning in agony, there will be tantrums, kicking and screaming, "No! I don't want to! I don't like this idea! NO!"

And maybe that will be okay, too.

The days of chemotherapy that summer left me incapacitated. In addition to chemo, I was still recovering from major surgery, liver failure, poor nutrition. The chemotherapy poisoned every cell in my body; the faster the cells grew, the more they were poisoned. The doctors hoped that the fastest-growing tumor would take the worst hits from the treatment — but no one knew for sure if or for how long the chemo might work. The treatment also caused profound anemia, as it killed off the production of new red blood cells. For the first time, I knew and experienced what I'd seen in some of my own profoundly anemic patients: a hollow, weak feeling, caused by the lack of red blood cells to carry energizing oxygen in my body.

Fatigue doesn't even begin to describe the feeling of anemia; it felt like even my brain cells slowed down. I couldn't think as fast as I used to. The constant nausea and debilitating enervation of those days is difficult to describe — just sitting on the end of our family room couch, doing nothing else, took everything in me. Walking into the kitchen was a superhuman task. Holding a book and moving my eyes across the page was simply too much exertion. Even though others weren't aware, I knew all too well what it cost me to accomplish the most basic tasks.

Chris and Dan were having a hard time. All of a sudden, they had to fend for themselves. Mom was home, but she didn't look or act like Mom. I tried to remain part of the family, to keep things familiar — even to get angry the way I used to when the situation called for it. We started taking the boys to a child psychologist to help us — and them — deal openly with our trauma. Dan, barely five, didn't say much, but we noticed his insecurity, which manifested itself in sleep walking and night terrors. Chris, age eight, could verbally express some of his fear and anger, and it helped. He even got to the point where he could say, "I hate that cancer in you," instead of saying, "I hate you."

From my journal:

> *"Cease striving and know that I am God." My strength and striving has always been through my intellect, which*

is what I've desperately clung to as a source of life. Now I've realized that I can't even strive enough to think my way to God. Even that is dramatically set aside for now. So what have I discovered? The same thing as always: God is with me, and I know Him here, in this awful place of suffering.

Before, I always said, "The horror is somewhere over there — and God stands between me and the horror, and I am not undone." Somehow, some people must have heard me saying, "I am not feeling any fear," which was not the case, even then. I am learning to lean closer to the fear, and to hear God saying, "I am here with you, with My arms around you."

"Why is it still so scary?" I ask. Then God says, "Because it is, it really is scary. There are some hard, almost impossible things to come, and you will suffer, and your anguish will be felt by Me, for I love you. And at the end of this time of sorrow, you will come with Me, beautiful daughter, and all tears will be wiped away. The sorrow is great but it cannot outweigh the weight of the joy of what I am doing."

Another thought: I am so glad I have time to prepare to die. To enjoy the gifts of the simple life, to move into others' lives, to speak of real things, to speak love to Mom, Ron, Chris, and Dan. There is so much I do not want to leave, but by grace I can say, "Thank You for what is. There is time to know and worship You here."

❧ *Nine* ❧

SIX WEEKS after my surgery, I returned to my work as a doctor part-time. Dr. K., my doctor, encouraged me to resume doing productive and familiar routines, so I went to work for three hours a day, wearing my wig. I timed my doctoring to the rhythm of the chemo, so that there were only two days every three weeks that I was too sick to leave home.

The first week after chemo was the hardest, but I made it through sheer will power. The second week was awful, too, but I experienced a noticeable improvement. The third week was marginal; I began to have some semblance of normalcy. Yet this was usually the week I suffered from anemia. If my red blood cell count dipped too low, I would have a blood transfusion. As a doctor, I knew full well the deadly risks of multiple transfusions, but I learned to adore the almost instant feeling of well-being I experienced from them.

That summer, I experienced enforced rest and struggle, along with the constant need for Ron's help. He did so much to pick up the slack, to keep our family life moving along with some semblance of normalcy. The big surprise for me was that I needed help from everyone: from the boys, our parents, neighbors, people at church — and I discovered people *wanted* to help. As a doctor, I was used to being the helper, and I was amazed at all the people who reached out to help me, for no particular reason at all.

I was unable to comprehend what some of them told me — that this story, *my* story, touched them deeply. I heard stories of people everywhere praying for me — everyone from a Little League team in Florida to a tiny new church in Romania.

Sometimes virtual strangers would express to me their own sense of vulnerability. It might have had something to do with our two young boys or the fact that I myself was a physician and healer. Whatever the case, it constantly amazed me that people would reach out to me rather than doing the "sensible" thing — to awkwardly withdraw.

As I reflect now, it seems the "sensible" thing for me would have been to lapse into bitterness and despair. Most of my life as a doctor had been based on performance and accomplishment, and I wondered what I would discover about myself when I could do nothing. Yet, as each day passed, I experienced something surprising: in the midst of my sickness and fright, I found great peace and joy. It was a time of humility. I found I could do very little, while at the same time I was being offered much by others. I found that I was released from the burden of "measuring up."

The grace I felt was this: now that I had neither a choice nor a chance, now that I had no capacity to do anything, I experienced joy instead of despair. Perhaps for the first time in my life I found I had great worth to God. My worth had to be found apart from performing, because I could literally do nothing. All I could do was to trust God absolutely and to rest in that trust. And it was then I experienced a revelation: all God had ever wanted from me was simply that — to trust and to rest. Nothing more.

But I didn't experience just "straightforward trusting" either. One of my cardinal rules as a doctor was "never snoop into your own medical chart," yet I broke that rule — and it was one of the hardest things I'd ever experienced. I read a letter written to my doctor about my cancer. The writer of the letter casually commented that, "as we know, these tumors are, unfortunately, 'uniformly aggressive.'" I carried that phrase around in my mind for days. It was a widely known fact. Always. No exception. Aggressive. This mindless, evil disease was out to dispose of me, and it was already part of me; it was strong and relentless and it would not be deterred. These thoughts held me captive for days until some dear friends prayed for me.

I found that I was most frightened when I couldn't

keep the same pace everyone else did, when I discovered I was being left behind. That summer, on the Fourth of July, I missed my traditional "fireworks night" with the boys. I admitted aloud that it was probably physically impossible for me to drive, park, carry belongings, walk, sit, and then head home for this evening outing. While I was fretting over the situation, Ron suddenly ferried the boys away, even though he hates fireworks. Later on he confirmed what I had feared: he was struggling to keep from emotionally "letting go" too soon. That night he lost the struggle — and reacted as if I were already out of the picture. But sometimes I wanted to let go too soon, too. We found that, by being able to express our feelings openly, we were able to get back on track together.

Once, I actually got to the point of literally screaming in frustration over not being able to *do,* to be a mom. For Chris's ninth birthday party, we took a gaggle of boys all day to Water World. That's a lot of hills and sun and heat and crowds, but we wanted to do something really special for Chris. I plopped myself down in a small patch of shade at the bottom of a hill and watched the smaller kids play in the little pool. Ron took the bigger boys, including Chris, across the park to a big ride. Then Chris started to get a sunburn, so he and his best buddy came and found me, hoping I'd have Chris's shirt.

But the shirt was at the top of the large hill — and we were at the bottom. I couldn't get the little kids out of the pool, and I couldn't leave them. I couldn't physically climb the hill to get the shirt, and I couldn't send Chris alone to get his own shirt. Chris was too old to stay with the little kids, and too young to go back alone through the crowd to find his dad. And when Chris insisted on trying to find Ron anyway, I couldn't even stop him.

So, in the middle of Water World, I screamed at the top of my lungs, "I can't do this!" I couldn't protect Chris from the sun or from being alone. What I felt when I screamed was this: I was furious at Chris for going, and furious at Ron for the position I was in, furious at my limitations, and furious to find myself standing in the middle of Water World, screaming.

From my journal:

> *I woke up screaming at God: "You have done this to me! You want me this way.... You want me ugly, dumb, and filthy ... no hair, body wide and weak, awkward, no mental or social graces for loveliness or to even think of You or to be a fragrance....*
>
> *"I cannot work, I make poor judgments at home, things disappear. I am fuzzy and without the person I knew as me. You have taken away me — now how can I praise You if there is not me? How can I hide in You if I am no longer me? Now that I am in this place I am really mad. You made me filthy, stinky, repugnant, disgusting,*

offensive, urine-soaked, with a sharp, get-away smell. Why did You do this to me?"

I know that without faith it is impossible to please God, and that I need to know that He is and that He is a rewarder of those who seek Him. But I don't. I cry out over and over, "Show me that You are — beyond my logic."

The next month, in August, I faced my inability to "do" in yet a different way. We had driven back to the Midwest on a "last visit" to see everyone in both our families — all the aunts, uncles, and cousins we had, as well as our parents. I was suffering the double effects of chemotherapy and severe anemia, and somehow there didn't seem to be enough of me to do what I wanted to do. People didn't want to talk about the cancer; they weren't ready to say the last things that needed to be said. Maybe I wasn't ready either, even though I never expected to see any of them again.

One day we went to a small amusement park on the lake near my cousin's home in Indiana. It was an all-day event with Grandma and Grandpa, the boys, Ron, and my cousin and her kids. Even though I took it easy, by afternoon I was exhausted. Just as I was leaving for a rest, Chris took my hand and said, "Let's go on the Ferris wheel, Mom. Take me on the Ferris wheel." I had to say, "I can't do it. I can't go with you." It broke my heart. Somehow that moment represented all the moments I would not be able to be with him when he wanted me. On the ride back to my cousin's house I started weeping to myself, and by the time I got there I was sobbing, "I can't do it. I can't be what you need, Chris."

But the story doesn't end there. Later, in the cool of the evening, I returned to the park, joined the family, and took that Ferris wheel ride with Chris. It felt good. I was relieved other people had been with him the rest of the afternoon when I could not.

I see now that it was good to feel the real pain that I had, to feel it in a real, healthy, unmistakable way. There was a part of me that grieved for my family and the fact that I knew I would leave them someday — and cause a hole in their lives. Despite my utter faith that God would take care of them and provide for them, as well as work such an experience for good into the fabric of their lives, I still knew that the loss would be real, and that the hole would be sad.

I didn't often allow myself to touch this real sadness. Even though other people were with Chris at the amusement park and he did get to go on the Ferris wheel, I learned I could still grieve the changes I was experiencing, and the sadness I felt at not being part of his life. Even though I knew that, someday, my family's loss would come, I knew when it did it would probably feel way too soon. And I mourned that.

At the same time, I often felt as if I were ready to slip away from this life. Before I had experienced the cancer, I had feared death — but when it finally stared me in the face, I saw it as an adventure, a real-life adventure. It seemed oddly paradoxical: to experience more of real life when I was just beginning to face death. But that is exactly what happened. I was beginning the final, common journey that each person must take. That, in itself, was adventure enough.

At the same time, I was also having more of an adventure in living. In a strange way, I finally felt free to live, knowing that I would soon die. I had never been a person to take a chance, to walk close to the edge of a deep canyon. But since I already found myself teetering on the brink, I began to take risks. I dreamed of other kinds of work, and I talked to other people openly about life and death and God.

From my journal:

This was the dream I had last night: it was a breezy, dark night and I was standing by a flagstone or limestone wall, just standing, trying to figure out what to do next. Somehow I seemed to be missing an appointment. I thought to myself, maybe I am at the wrong place, but it doesn't feel like the wrong place. I had been busy all day, so it felt restful just to be standing next to this warm, sandy-colored, kind-of-smooth-yet-rough-and-bumpy wall.

I had to reach my hands up and out a little, perhaps to catch the breeze or to reach out and touch the wall, but

I ended up holding them in front of me. Then I noticed glistening gossamer forming, moonlight trailing flowers up and around and out of my hands, cascading down and around. They were beautiful, glistening with subtlety, softly fragrant. They provided me a beautiful veil.

Then the wall took on the appearance of a grotto, and the gossamer covering spread to every nook and cranny. I still stood there, enjoying and waiting. My hands lowered to my sides, and I touched something, still light-filled and gossamer, but much bigger and warmer. It was a large farm horse, friendly and attached by a lead to my hand . . . and another horse at my other side. It was clear to me they'd be pleased if I had any sugar cubes with me — and sure enough, in the pockets of my long, flowing dress were the desired objects.

The horses began to move . . . we were going somewhere. I walked at first . . . but wondered to myself, who is the other horse for? I found myself riding then. And I looked, and it was my Lord riding with me, and on His robe and thigh was a name written that no one knew but He. We were going home. The wedding feast of the Lamb was prepared. The moonlight darkness was exquisite and haunting — but we were headed toward the day.

❧ *Ten* ❧

T HE HARDEST PART of my journey toward the edge occurred in the fall, when Dr. K. wanted to stop chemotherapy. I went a little crazy. Early on, she'd called leading cancer experts around the country to confirm her diagnosis of what drugs to use and how to use them. Since I had such a rare form of cancer, no one knew what to expect from any treatment. Frankly, no one expected much.

From the beginning, in planning our next step of treatment, Dr. K. would always say, "*If* the tumor responds to chemotherapy." She'd already informed me the chemo was not a cure — that eventually the tumor cells would "figure it out" and start pumping out poison as fast as it was pumped in.

I started praying that the cancer cells would become stupid and never figure out how to grow insensitive to the treatment. But I had noticed that my hair was growing back, even while I was in chemo — and as much as I enjoyed it, I knew it wasn't a good sign. If mild-mannered hair could figure out how to grow back, how about vicious cancer cells?

We'd base our decision on whether or not to continue chemo on a recent CT liver scan. If the cancer was shrinking, we'd continue treatment. If it remained the same, then perhaps only scar tissue was left, or maybe unresponsive cancer. One Friday, knowing that Dr. K. would be looking at the scan, I called her office and left a very explicit message that I needed to hear from her that day, before the weekend arrived.

By late afternoon, she hadn't called. I called back and discovered she was already gone, and she would be away most of the next week. I was deeply distressed. How could she leave me untreated for that many days? I had visions of tumor cells dividing away, reaching some critical mass — or traveling somewhere new in my body, where they would multiply, uncontainable. Her partner heroically called me back, listened to my hysterics, and patiently tried to explain the facts to me. It was then I began to realize it didn't really matter what they did: what they'd "gotten" through this treatment was all they'd "get," and what was left was going to be left. No cure. In fact, my treatment was over.

It was at that point I truly learned about trust. As much as I'd been trusting God and feeling peaceful, I found out just what was really going on in my heart. I hadn't thought I'd been trusting in the treatment — but I found out I certainly didn't want there to be *no* treatment. I amused even myself as I tried every convoluted way imaginable to obtain a different final answer. I pestered my doctor for more chemotherapy. I went to the large university hospital for other opinions. The answer was always the same: it won't help.

I would ask leading questions like, "Do you think we should plan our big once-in-a-lifetime family vacation for this October, or should we take it next October, when I won't feel sick from the chemo?" Dr. K. was wise and immovable and would only answer, "Do what you think best. Do what you have to do." She never hedged by giving me false hope, nor did she steal from me true hope. Her answers gave me the solidity I needed to face reality: I was dying. Now, I was not simply standing near the edge of the precipice; I was taking a step over. The message, from all sides, was clear: "There is nothing more that can be done for you." *Now* it was time to talk about trust.

I began living day by day. I knit afghans for my two boys, so they'd have something from me to wrap around themselves. My mother-in-law promised to finish the Christmas stocking I was making for Dan if I couldn't.

One day Ron and I went out to lunch — and caught the waitress eavesdropping on our strange table conversation: what to do with dead bodies. I surprised the oncology psych-support nurse by asking for information on preparing to die, and she surprised me back: no one had ever asked her that question before.

I didn't buy next year's appointment book.

My best friend, Dottie, really struggled. She didn't want me to leave. I shared with her that, even though I'd only reached the edge of dying, I had worked so hard and come so far that I didn't want to do it over again. It was too scary. So I asked her, please, not to want me to get well too much. Two other wise and wonderful people who'd discipled me over the years also discussed dying with me — and did so without trying to "reassure" me out of my sentiments. They helped open my heart up to both possibilities of God working — dying or living. Sometimes, it was harder to hold onto the idea of my living, but my friends firmly held the door open for me. They very gently and very definitely challenged me to stay connected to this life, to trust God with my living as well as my dying — whether I stayed on earth five days, five months, five years, or fifty years. "So hold on," they encouraged me. And I did.

Some people were offended that I didn't seem to fight or rage or struggle or hate the process more. They thought I was giving up. Still others thought I wasn't trusting God enough because I wasn't claiming a full healing, by faith. But, as I look back now, they didn't understand. I've never believed death is "right." It's not what God meant or designed for us. We're not created for this. We hate it. Our very hatred and wish to negate it tell us that it is a great wrong. In fact, I believe death is stupid and ridiculous.

No, I *was* fighting plenty hard. And I was trusting plenty hard, too. The reason I wasn't raging, hating, struggling, or claiming healing promises is because I knew I couldn't afford to fill my heart and life with the bitterness it would take to generate that kind of rage. Frankly, I felt small inside. I simply didn't feel big enough to fight — but I did trust a God who was big enough. I knew Him to be true, and to be the Healer, and that seemed to be enough for me. In fact, what surprised me most in knowing He was the Healer was being able to grasp that truth apart from whether or not He healed me. It felt like a profound discovery. Knowing God in the midst of sorrow meant "healing" to me. It was a taste of eternal life in the now, and it was mine.

So if I wasn't struggling, then what could I do? These were five things that came to mind, things I determined to do:

- to keep my face turned toward Jesus' face ...

- to keep people in this world connected to me ...

- to trust my own instincts about what it meant to "cope," instead of worrying about doing it the "right" way . . .

- to refuse to be defined by the disease, but instead to realize everything God created me to be . . .

- to participate fully in the full traditional medical treatments available — to not chase after every "possible cure," but to trust God to do the work of His choosing.

So, when people asked me, "How are you doing?" my best and truest answer, whether I felt good or bad, could always be, "I am doing well."

From my journal:

I read in Matthew today that argument with the Sadducees, "Whose wife of the seven will she be in heaven?" It says she will be no one's wife, that all of our ecstasies and intimacies will be with God in heaven. That really got me crying. Will I die and give up Ron? Will I walk away without remembering? That's too sad and scary for me. I know Ron. I don't know God that well yet. I don't want to trade relationships.

I am scared, really, to leave this earth and to go away with God. It feels like an abusive situation that I'm required to enter or, at the very least, an unknown one. Will Ron be left behind knowing that I have forgotten him and that there will be no reunion of our exclusive relationship in heaven? What a loss.

When I think too hard I cry, am scared, torn apart by emotion. In another place in Matthew it says to embrace suffering. Am I not embracing? Yet it's so hard when my heart feels like it is ripping apart.

✑ *Eleven* ✑

OUR FAMILY DID, indeed, go on our big dream vacation that fall. It became something to focus on
and aim for: "If I can just make it until our vacation...."
Then, when the big event came and went, I was left
baffled. The time that stretched out before me seemed
too unstructured, too random — and I began to wonder if the goal of our vacation was all that had kept me
alive. But by Christmas, my condition was still stable.
I began to get familiar with no changes in my monthly
check-ups, no detection of any growing cancer spots.

In fact, during this time, I began having the impres-
sion I was healed, yet I shared it with only one person.
Two other people, whom I didn't know well, were con-
vinced I was healed — and that God had told them
so. I didn't know what to do with that information. I'd
known faithful, godly people who were absolutely con-
vinced God would heal them, right up until the day they
died. So it was very confusing to me. I didn't know what
to do with my own notion I was healed, much less the
convictions of the other two people.

After a while, I began to live week to week. My first tentative act of living was that I bought a personal appointment calendar for the new year and a new, complicated needlework project to work on (after the current complicated project was finished). I appeared in public with new extremely short, silver, but my-very-own hair. People commented I looked beautiful.

But for the next several months, besides occasionally filling in part-time for other physicians, I frittered my time away. Mostly I played Nintendo and computer games with — and without — the boys. I fretted about how I'd feel someday, when I realized I'd squandered precious time. But, somehow, I couldn't help it.

From my journal:

Good Friday, 1993:

One year today I have lived with my own mortality —
in all its sweetness and terror. What do I feel? First,
grateful — even grateful that I feel gratitude and not
bitterness. I also feel peaceful, despite the fact that what
I feared so much, which I knew I would face sooner or
later, is here — and it is sooner rather than later.

I also feel anxious about my work and our income,
anxious that people are drawing away from me. I do feel
reconnected with Ron, which comforts me.

I've found myself wondering if I fought and hated,
would I discover just how frightened and angry I really

am? Would I waste my remaining days in bitterness and helplessness? I don't want to waste any more time. No, I don't want to make the focus of my life hating cancer. . . .

Yesterday I lost control. My car was smoking, and shortly thereafter I determined that my latest work contract left me with $100 after two days of work last month. I cancelled a politically correct meeting, and I've been thinking about attributing it all to lack of estrogen, as opposed to the cancer. I'm wondering if it is more noble, mature, spiritual to ignore these crazy emotions and to continue on as best I can — or is it all right to focus on me, face what is there, and trust God with this, too — perhaps "lean into" the feelings? I wish I knew.

How do I know I am starting to get well, to turn the corner? Water does not taste bitter . . . some food tastes very good . . . I am writing here . . . I am on my feet more . . . I did the dishes yesterday . . . stopped my husband on the stairs this morning . . . I am writing notes to friends. . . .

Later in the day:

I went with Chris this morning on a field trip to the play "Wizard of Oz." And I have been crying all afternoon . . . why? Chris asked me to go for two reasons. One, he knows I like the story, and, two, he wanted to sit by me. What mother could resist that request? I rescheduled my CT scans which were supposed to be today, and I drove the car for the first time in a long time, and

I endured the twenty-minute school bus ride and then the long walk around the high school to get to the theater door. I could not let being sick prevent me from saying yes to Chris. But I still felt terrible.

Chris kept watching me. Once he took my hand. While I was walking back to the bus, I couldn't keep up with him and the class. Chris kept looking over his shoulder, keeping an eye on me so I wouldn't get lost or get on the wrong bus. Maybe that is where the tears come from. . . . It was hard and scary.

In May, a new spring, I'd finished eight months of being off chemotherapy. Dr. K. slipped up one day and described me as, "A person who has *had* cancer." She then changed the phrase to "Who has inactive cancer." But I heard that slip.

We were moving to a new house, and it became an important process for me to sort through all our things, to touch everything with my own hands, to put each item in its place, to identify beloved objects. I cleared the house of useless items, and I cleaned out my files, discarding things that weren't interesting to me. I found that I crossed some sort of invisible line back into living again. Even though I knew that, at any moment, the illness could return, I did not feel ill. I was living a couple of months at a time.

One way I knew that I had "crossed the line" back into the land of the living was that I suddenly wanted to do meaningful work. I wanted to feel more and to grieve better, and I wanted to express all of who God has created me to be, to honor God by "filling out my edges" more. I became occupied with the business of living, not dying, even though I knew that when I faced death next time around, the process would be harder.

∽ Twelve ∽

I T'S TAKEN A WHILE for me to finish writing this part
of my story, almost two years. Maybe I was so busy
living it that I couldn't take the time or energy to think
about it, or maybe I just feel safer now. During my "living months," I dove into new kinds of work, assisting
other physicians and medical systems in dealing with the
variety of huge changes in the industry. I explored more
of who I was in the work world.

I didn't work full time, but that was good. In my clin-
ical practice, I felt a deeper empathy, a more humble,
admiring, respectful, trusting empathy for my patients
and for what they'd experienced. A lot of people asked
me if that aspect of my medical practice changed, and
it did.

We settled into the new house, and the boys no longer
felt like the rookies at the new school. Instead of buying
a one-level home to accommodate my future illness, we
decided to purchase a five-level home that we loved. Ron
and I talked about our plans for the next year, yet sometimes we hesitated with an unspoken "if" between us.

The boys still referred to the time that I was bald. When any one of us was sick, even our pet dog, the boys would ask if that one was going to die. And my youngest son, Dan, age six, became much more of a lap-sitter and hugger with me. Maybe it was just his personality or perhaps a phase in childhood development, but I couldn't help wondering if he finally felt it was safe enough to draw close again to a mom who might leave him and go away.

My situation really did not change. The cancer is, in all likelihood, only currently inactive. At any moment, I could be dealing again with every feeling I've written about in this book. I realize that, now, I've crossed back into the land of living, but I am still within sight of the edge of death. Yet, for now, I know that I have walked for a time in the valley of the shadow, and I found Jesus walking with me; peace instead of terror, meaning instead of chaos, and life, not death. At the times I had the least hope of much future in this world, I found the present moment filled with richness and glory. I experienced living in the present moment as much as anyone ever has, and I didn't feel deprived. I had a sure sense of the continuity of life that would extend beyond the boundaries of dying.

Even so, I am grateful to be living — yet I'm surprised by some of the complexities of still being here. I do not understand why I am still alive. Even now, I don't allow

Ron to tell me how much the illness has cost us financially. I have to fight against the feeling that I need to do something grand and wonderful to justify my continued existence. The risk I face in surviving is that, as many of my natural capabilities return, I will be tempted to try to do things for God instead of simply continuing to trust Him.

God gave me great blessing in the midst of great danger. I knew He was trustworthy, He was the Healer, He found me worthy, and He was with me, and I knew I could do nothing. I found something of His peace and joy in the midst of sorrow and fear, and both the joy and the sorrow were greater and more real. His joy does not make the sorrow disappear; it makes the sorrow bearable and makes us able to bear more. In fact, now the tears can finally flow for the child within me who hurt. The joy permits the sorrow to be more real, not less, and our response can be to heal and grow, not to shut down.

I am grateful to the Lord for allowing me to face a situation in which there was no choice. I had to trust Him. It took the threat of death to do so, but it still happened. I found Him trustworthy apart from the circumstances. In the middle of the worst circumstances I had ever faced, I knew the joy and peace that trusting Him is.

Now I happen to have better circumstances, but I still do not want anything in my life to stand in the way of my trusting Him: whatever still lurks in my past, whatever sorrows and fears I've still refused to face, whatever I've chosen to handle apart from trusting God. I desire to come before Him with all of who I am, and trust Him. I have had a taste of life trusting God, and I want more. For me, the rock-bottom issue is knowing God, whether I live or die.

Part II

THE PILGRIMAGE HOME

✏ *Thirteen* ✏

A GLORIOUS SUNRISE this morning. I had just sat down to quiet reading, writing, thinking, and computer work when Chris came downstairs. He sat with me a bit, even leaned on me. He wants to do something fun today. We talked about going to a movie....

I awakened this morning without gut pain. But I have a bad right trapezoid trigger point, which I think means something is awry inside. I expect the gut pain to return. I have a sense of fullness, just about where my liver is. I have been going out without my wig — even though my hair isn't quite long enough to look really decent. No gut pain yet, sitting in my chair. Thank God. I'd like to sit, make meals, go to the movies and the grocery store.

During the day, the pain came back. I'm writing this and waiting for the doctor at the same time. I called the doctor, but I've received no call back. I am somewhat anxious that Dr. K. has something to tell me. I can feel right upper quadrant discomfort with deep breathing, but it is mild. Even with the pain, I don't feel that sick. I try to tell myself it is not the cancer.

I saw something beautiful this morning — the water I poured over the little cactus in the east kitchen window caught in beads on the ends of some of the cactus spines. The sun shone through — making them like gemstones or tiny stars. Now I think about the morning dewy cobwebs I have seen in my life, and how fortunate I am to have seen them. Was it at the farm? Girl Scout camp? The redwood forests or the preserves? All places of beauty.

I stumbled across something this afternoon I'd never seen before: a PBS show called "The Gift of Painting." I took it to mean "a gift given to those who would try it." Just a watercolor bowl and peaches, but the painter explained a lot of what she was doing as she was painting. I found myself saying, "This isn't real art, I don't have supplies, I can't draw even the basics," but I watched it anyway. I think I might try to watch it and try painting something. Just doing what she was doing might not really be "creating" for me, but it would be the *process* I'd enjoy. Feeling it.

Ron's spoken concern for me right now is that I am doing all right emotionally. We are both in limbo again, it seems.

I am hurled out of sleep at 3:00 a.m. and forcefully compelled to get out of bed. I hope it's God waking me up, although it could just be drugs or anxiety. The rules have changed since yesterday. I now have cancer that cannot be treated. I now have cancer that no longer stays somewhat courteously in one spot. Some comment was made by the doctor about the gallbladder not looking right — maybe that's part of my pain.

I called Ron first thing. We had the same quality conversation — quiet. I think we are talking a month to two weeks . . . even less. I have so much to say, so much to prepare, so much to say and to do for my boys and Ron. We haven't told the boys yet. I had a good evening with them, but tomorrow we will start a new family chapter.

✑ *Fourteen* ✑

Nancy's cancer returned in November 1994, and it quickly spread to her brain. She endured high doses of steroids, along with radiation, during this time.

I REMEMBER CONFESSING in the first part of this story that I had been healed. I felt that I had crossed some sort of line into the land of the well and the living. On one level, I was comfortable with having my bags packed, since I was ready to leave soon, but at another level I reentered this world by crossing over that line and feeling well. I resented the words, "You are in remission." This time around, I haven't felt that way, nor do I expect I will in the future.

This time around, although I haven't felt like I've actually been dying, I haven't felt healed or well. I haven't reentered life on those terms. I expect to be feeling sick again, and in some way, it makes me sick now. I have ongoing, present-condition cancer as I have never had it before. That is the minor key symphony playing in the background.

What are my bags like now? Once they were neatly packed. Now the stuff is still in them, but they are open and jumbled and all in a mess. I could not get started on my journey now very quickly or easily. Everything I have would have to be stuffed in and the locks forced closed before I could pick up those bags and move down the road again. It reminds me of the regret I feel when our family trashes the hotel rooms we stay in on vacation. I keep thinking it would be so nice for everything to remain orderly and to look lovely.

Reading the Gospel of Mark, I think about Peter's mother being healed — and how she immediately gets up to make dinner for her guests. Again, the knowledge comes to me of what a gift it is to be able to serve others. I ask God to heal me of whatever is fever in me and to restore to my use the gifts He's already given me to be able to serve others.

From my journal:

> *Would I go mad if I faced the illness without God? This time around I feel more of the sorrow, the terror. . . . I feel as if I've been struck by an abusive blow — a slap so hard-handed that it sends me back across the room, into the wall and onto the floor. I feel without defense, and I wonder: what is coming next? At one level, I feel*

like the abuse is from God — at least He is not changing my circumstances. He is allowing it. I am suffering, and defenseless, and it feels like abuse.

Yet, at the same time, I trust Him. I trust that I can ask the wonderful question, "Do You love me?" without any demand, and that He will answer me someday. I rest in that now. I know I desire more time and to feel good enough to put the house in order for Ron and the boys, to prepare words of love for Dan and Chris, to wrap up important business, and to say what I can to others about this illness — but I don't know if all that will happen. Right now, I don't even know how close those desires are to a demand. I'm praying for the Spirit to keep my heart soft, trusting, receiving, embracing. This is the heart I desire: to be able to say to God, "I desire Your presence, but I don't demand it. I desire understanding of Your purpose in my life and in others' lives, but I don't demand it. I desire to know that I am representing You well, impacting others on Your behalf, but I don't demand it. I desire that whatever is foolishness, whatever prevents me from knowing, hearing, seeing, and sensing You, would be revealed to me — but I don't even demand that."

I trust in Your darkness.

Thank You, God, for the specific Scripture in Luke that I read today that clearly says I must not concern myself with how many or how few are saved. When I am tempted by this concern, I want to ask the Spirit to remind me of this. . . .

It is somehow a great encouragement to me to know that God's face is turned toward all of us. It's then that I know I have his full attention, kind of like when you ask your child, "Look at me when I'm speaking to you!" These are verses I've drawn comfort in, that have reminded me to look full-faced to Him:

1 Chronicles 16:11, "Look to the Lord and His strength. Seek His face always."

Psalm 27:8, "My heart says of you, 'Seek His face.' Your face, Lord, I will seek."

Numbers 6:24–26, "The Lord bless you and keep you. The Lord make His face shine upon you and be gracious to you; The Lord turn His face toward you and give you peace."

I know I've found this peace to be indescribable at my times of greatest need.

✦ *Fifteen* ✦

I T TOOK ALL DAY, a day of planning, negotiating, arranging, contriving, but by six o'clock I knew I could do it: I knew I had the stamina, the permission, the technical support (IVs and all that stuff) to make it to Chris's state fair presentation at school. I had thought for sure that I couldn't go — that the disease would say "no" to him one more time. In fact, he had even taken the initiative and had said, "Mom, I don't think you can make it. You would have to stand during the whole presentation, so that's all right. Don't worry about it." Chris has tried so hard to take good care of me; I just want to take good care of him, too.

Yet I got the bright idea of obtaining a therapeutic pass during the morning — and the entire oncology department got the same idea, too! So I drove to school with Dottie, who had come to see me earlier in the morning.

When I walked in, the fifth graders were singing patriotic songs. Then, suddenly, Dan saw me — and he got this incredible look on his face. He said, "Mom, what are you doing here?" The next thing he asked was, "You don't get to go home, do you?" I said, "No, I can only be here a little while, and then I have to go back to the hospital. I just wanted to be here so much." So we sat together on a little camp chair, with his arms around me, and we talked and laughed and commented. He told me the job he had in Chris's booth, and that the state of Wisconsin (one of the exhibits) was giving away Oscar Meyer Weiner whistles.

Then Chris came out. He looked so good in his costume — Dottie said it was one of the best ones there: dark vest with bright yellow piping, a sunflower bow tie and a mustard yellow shirt. He just looked so spiffy, and he glued those people to his booth — stood there and told amazing stories about Kansas. I just know he is going to do something with speaking someday.

He was so happy to see me. I know he didn't expect me to come, and I gave him a big hug and told him what a great job he'd done. This time, the disease didn't win, didn't tell him "no" one more time.

I came back to the hospital, tired and tearful, but also deeply happy. God gave me something by allowing me to be there, by seeing Chris and Dan's responses, by loving them that way. It was right — and the right is good and the good is joyful, and I was peaceful.

Later that night, my friend Pat called. She asked me, "What hope do you have? What is your hope?" And I told her I had a hope of heaven so huge that it felt like I had no questions about it, no fear at all of being there. I told her, overall, my hope is pretty simple. I don't have to be an overachieving physician anymore, although I grieve that loss. I know I don't have to be that person anymore — I just have to live more richly with the people who are important to me. "And you're one of those people, Pat," I told her. She thanked me. It was a wonderful moment.

∽ Sixteen ∽

I SAW TWO identical hats today — blue denim, floppy-brimmed things, the front of each caught up in a sizeable silk flower and raffia bow.

The hats were identical, but not the women who wore them. One hat crowned a pale face. At first glance, there was something out of proportion in this woman's overall look. Ah! — no hair, just hat. She was older than I (just a little), and pleasant, but with a washed-out, beaten-up look about her.

But then, each of us in that room carried the same look. We were all there for chemotherapy — poison to kill the killer that had entered our lives. We all had the look, and we all had no hair, not even eyelashes. Three women wore scarves. I had my wig.

She had the hat.

The second hat showed up outside the chemotherapy room. It was at my son's elementary school field day.

I watched from the sidelines. It had taken my utmost effort to walk each step from the parking lot to the field, and to slowly set up my little folding chair. I planned to sit for a few minutes and watch my son. It meant a lot to him to have Mom there, and it meant a lot to me to give him that gift, the mom who watches. I do not think he knew what it cost me in physical endeavor to come and watch him, yet his eyes kept coming back to find me watching. That was good enough.

I glanced around. There was the hat! This time it was perched on the head of a young mother. Dark hair framed her face and fell to her shoulders. She was lining up twenty-five first graders for tug-of-war, with lots of energy, lots of laughter, and a loud whistle.

Suddenly, I found myself twisting away from the scene with my eyes shut. I wept. How could she be wearing the same hat and yet be so different? Was it too painful or too wonderful to bear? I wasn't sure at first. She was all energy, movement, play. Just standing there was effortless for her, requiring hardly a thought to make it happen.

I remembered a time like that, when my body was just part of me, a part that would do what I wanted. Now I lived estranged from my body, a body that would not go far, or fast, or long, no matter what I wished. At first all I wanted was to be back to that time, when I was my body and the world was easy.

But almost immediately, I found myself thanking God. I thanked Him that she stood there in the midst of the children, so easy, so unaware. Unlike me, she did not yet seem to know that the world had fallen into what it was never meant to be, what it should not be. Her innocence was good. That she could live in innocence was good. Like the first Creation, "It was good." It was a little taste of Eden still in this world; maybe a little taste of heaven. I started cheering for the tug-of-war game and for this mom with her hat. Thank God! Let this glimpse of heaven be woven wonderfully into this world. Let this hat and her heart continue.

In that brief moment I also thanked God for the hat on the woman in the chemotherapy room. That hat had brought grace and comfort, gently covering a shameful nakedness. The ugliness of the disease is not right; it is not meant to be, but it is. I do not want to be in the chemotherapy room, but I am.

I know with every bit of my being that this disease is wrong, and in contrast, I know God is Right. God intended and created good. He Himself is good. He is health. He is everything opposite to the illness that now walks with me. I have these as gifts — realities that exist unshaken, and thankfulness.

The blows of life have come to that chemotherapy room. I can see it in the other women's eyes, and they see it in mine. But also there has come the preciousness of life. How else would I know the unique beauty of each hat, even though both might look exactly the same?

From my journal:

A letter to my best friend, Dottie:
I am going to try to tell you how precious your tears have been to me. Of all the things you have ever given

me, said to me, or done for me, those tears were the greatest. They were most precious to me because they gave me you, and what I need and love most is you. Thank you for your tears. I want you to know and believe this because I know you don't like your tears, and although I rejoice that you gave them to me, I am also afraid that you will want to take them back and hide them.

This really is a serious, mysterious, scary, bad situation I find myself in. If you don't let yourself feel it and cry when you need to, then I find myself in the situation alone. If we cry and hug and hang onto each other, and to God, then we are there in the serious, mysterious, scary situation together, and then it is not so bad. So in spite of how hard it is for you to cry, and in spite of how much you hate it, I welcome your coming to share your tears with me.

Did you hear what you said as you started to weep? You said, "I don't want to cry because it will upset you." Those are words of long ago, words for your own survival. But they are not words for now, not words for me and you. Your tears were life-giving and life-saving to me. They kept me from being hard and tough and alone, and I am grateful.

Once, when I was describing to my counselor, Al, about how I had to "toughen up" early on to survive childhood, he said, "You must find it so strange to be among people who welcome and honor your grief and pain, and who do not flee from it." Strange is too mild a word. I have pondered his statement for a long time. Now I have had *a glimpse of understanding from the other side — for you, my beloved friend, give me the gift of yourself when you share your grief and pain and God's love. That is why your tears are welcomed, both for the joy of your awakening and the precious gift of yourself in my life.*

I love you,
Nancy

✍ Seventeen ✍

I AWOKE TO uncontrollable pain this morning. As soon as I sat upright it gripped me. It would have been unbearable for more than a few moments, yet not so bad as to make me cry out. Worse is still possible. I could not sleep, only drift in and out.

I hear wind. Must be a front. The sunset last night was gorgeous....

I was very fearful today, the first time in a week. Part of it was the growing stress the boys are showing. Dan shutting down, turning away, and Chris blowing up. I was able to spend an hour with a friend from the multiple sclerosis center. She cried with me, so sad, and said, "I think God wants you back, and He is not going to be dissuaded this time." Somehow that wasn't at all offensive to me. It was comforting. I offered that tears mean we were not meant for goodbyes. She gave me the gift of saying my life had given her something, something she hopes, when her time comes, to find in her life — and that is that she has seen me remain curious, open, and dignified. She said that was very rare.

I had a much more relaxed, approachable, fun time with Dan last night. We had a sword fight with — get this — string cheese sticks. Chris would not let me help him with math. He sent me away and I went. Ron and I were utterly enchanted with his science project: crystals. They were so sparkly after the solution was poured off. Chris asked me to break off the extra bottom crystals. Then he wanted to break the three stones apart. In doing so, the whole cluster slipped off one of the stones. He was heartbroken, sobbing wildly, "I wanted it to be perfect." I agreed with his grief, especially since you can't have it perfect in this world. His sorrow spills out, for more than just me. The core of his being is sorrow. Care for him so he knows it is You, Lord. Let him know being cared for.

I need the promise of renewed strength and soaring. Yesterday was the first day I had to decline previous engagements — too sick. I had nausea, profound fatigue, and increasing muscle aches. I slept most of the day and all night.

I feel content again this morning, not so frustrated by my lack of time for all my hopeful artistic projects.

If only all day could keep this "early morning potential" about it. Seems like anything and everything could get done.

Yesterday was doing only what I wanted to do, and that was mostly photo albums for Ron and the boys. I did make it all the way to the '87 Disneyland trip....I finished straightening the kitchen, called the hospice. Researched a data base, looking for a tape. Maybe today there will be a library visit for Dan. A grocery store visit. A menu starter.

From my journal:

> *I have sudden tears as I once again realize my brain is being affected. What will I become, and what have I become? I am scared, I am so scared. Of what? Losing myself, others losing me, being pitiful, being an affront to the kingdom, leaving, madness instead of beauty, emptiness that terrifies others, curses, blackness, dullness, self-centeredness....*
>
> *So how is it that I can stop crying at all? That all these things will be redeemed is too much to believe. Yes, I am very hurt and scared, and the pain is real now — even though in many ways I am all right. Even You, Lord, grieved in the Garden about what would be coming to You.*

It is this mysterious, inside world I want to speak of. What is familiar to me is lost, to a great extent. My world is soft, squishy, pushable, drifting at night. I feel like my mental space is too big somehow, and stuffed up inside with these squishy softnesses to roll and slide into. It's like wading into something a little thicker than water, like cotton candy marshmallow creme, cobwebs — but mental wading, wandering without direction or purpose. It's not unpleasant; it's just that it goes nowhere.

Before, I thought God wanted just my intellect. "There has to be way to figure this out and understand it," I thought. "I will know how to handle this....I am smarter than many....You will use me for my intelligence, I bet. I can integrate people and ideas....I will have an impact, either living or dying." But now I am stupid, simple, limited, thin, scared, much out-of-control, a mystery.

Yet Al, my counselor, says that the fragrance, the life-giving, is still there in my choices....I don't see it, but thank God he does.

I awoke at 6:30 a.m. and couldn't remember if I took any pain medication. I want to sleep, but I am suspicious of it — like the arctic explorer who must not fall asleep in the cold. The biggest thing that I did yesterday is that I threw out almost all my multiple sclerosis papers and grants. Goodbye. Goodbye. I won't be needing you anymore. Even if I got well, I would start fresh. A friend called last night, and she put something well: if this process was just about my life, instead of affecting others, we'd all be celebrating, dancing, jumping up and down. I'm almost there! Almost home. But the burden of suffering remains for those left who will miss me.

Another friend came by. She talked again to me of the importance of telling my story, to continue the wonderful, precious mystery of ordinary life. She gave me a poem she's written, done in beautiful, bright-colored calligraphy. She told me that she is not afraid of death now, because of me.

I think of James Earl Jones's character in the movie *Field of Dreams,* when he was invited into the corn field. He stuck his hand into the corn, watched it disappear — and drew it out quickly. Then he laughs, and looking into his friends' faces, he steps clear into the field. I think there will be some of that, when the time comes: a stepping into another plane.

What act of kindness did I do for myself today? I ate the leftover spaghetti and put lots of Parmesan cheese on it — and I will eat the rest tomorrow.

Read Daniel 3:17–18. If we are thrown into the blazing furnace, the God we serve is able to save us from it, and He will rescue us from the hand of the king. But even if He does not, we will not serve your god, or worship your golden image. Ron tells me he is depressed today. He knows as no other that I am not feeling well. He sees me working on final papers. I can only lean against him as I sit at the desk and he stands next to me. I can pray hard, and give him to You, God, give him to Your care. He reads others' words of love to me — their affirmations of who I am. He says tomorrow we will have time together. What can we do to make it an extraordinary time?

Ron asks me the important question: do you have any ideas for a final memorial service? He doesn't flinch. Yes, I do, I say. I have many ideas. That gave me great joy and comfort that I could soak up on many levels. Something amazing happened last night after Ron and I saw *Mr. Holland's Opus*. Ron drew some thoughts from his Sunday school teachings as well and told me he could never before fully understand what my passion for music had meant to me, but that now he had a glimpse. He said he wished he could have experienced it together alongside me. I could weep over that loss and also the loss of that part of my life with the boys. And conversely, I will never understand Ron's passion for sports. But to speak of it together was something I never thought would happen. Today has been a weepy, sleepy day. My hair is starting to come out.

It's night and we are with our friend, Harold, at his cabin. Wonderful stars. Waist-deep snow from where the car is parked to the cabin. Favorite pizza for dinner and multitudes of plans for tomorrow. ... It seems like the pages of my journal are more and more simple "ah-hahs," but I will just keep writing.

I got myself in a difficult spot this morning. I was sitting in a comfy rocker, soft wrapper and head gear, coffee at hand, pain pills nearby if I needed them, but I didn't. Then I started crying and there was no Kleenex in sight. ... I need to be doing paperwork and homework and fun things with the kids. Ron has already confided in me that, in the last week, he has seen losses in my thinking, a creeping dullness.

From my journal:

> *How do I feel? These last few days I have written during this morning time, when I am a little clearer mentally, perhaps. And what about this time feels so different? It is like being distant, somehow far off, apart from others' experience of the world. Like something is constantly "on" and sort of distracting in the background of my mind. There was no way I could see how to approach Chris's grade school math problem. And what happened to my box of pills? All of a sudden it was empty except for one pill. Surely I had the box filled for the week. So where did the last two days go?*

I see but do not receive the impact. I take in but do not find connections. I see Scripture, understand the concept of rest, but do not find the sweet peace because of the clamor within me — and I think it is brain dysfunction, not primarily spiritual. But I cannot get to God the way I think I used to: through reason. So it means trust without the experience of trust right now, simply because God is trustworthy.

I have many physical questions right now. Parts of me are not working. Is it more cancer? What about my spinal cord? Is it spreading to my brain? Why does my skin feel sensitive and irritated by touch almost all over? Will it turn into pain? Will I be paralyzed, incontinent? Absent mentally and emotionally?

Chris invites me to sit out on the porch step today, so I can watch him play basketball. It's a nice day, but it's windy. I go in for a jacket, then a hat. My new soft fleece outdoors hat . . . the best I have. Chris just ran out into the driveway chasing the ball, and looked up at me to see if I was looking at him. My kid inside is having fun. My grown-up inside wants a nap.

I remember my girlhood pony, Cherry. How special to have had a pony — a real, live, warm, roan, shaggy, bushy pony. I'm thinking about my loss of her, and how angry I was at the grownups. They could have done something to keep her from dying, but they didn't want to. That made all of their comforting words to me mean nothing. None brought real comfort. None even recognized my real sorrow. Lord, please show me that my children will experience something different from me, from Ron and grandparents, from friends — grown up or otherwise. I know I can talk to them ahead of time about what people might be capable of saying to them.

Ephesians 1:18: "I pray that the eyes of your heart might be enlightened in order to know the hope which he has called you to...." I pray that we are changed by higher, wider, deeper purposes, so that we can see what He is really calling us to. I'm thinking about what our friend, Tom, said last night, about people who pray for comfort and "good things," or for "getting over the bad things." Maybe the point isn't getting over the bad things, the suffering. Maybe the point is found in the midst of the suffering.

Every day I feel less well, although people say I look better. I think they are looking at me with the eyes of love. It is really windy today, very cold weather. February is heading us toward March's lion. I see a green floating color over this page as I am writing. I think it was yesterday, really, that I realized I am already too sick and unwell to play and have fun anymore. How sad — what a loss, when I had just come to the point of starting to claim that part of me, know it, enjoy it, see how I could give it as a gift to others.

The late afternoon sun lights me in the living room. It has been a lovely day, although I have only been out once. I'm antsy for the boys to come home. I don't want anything to happen or to be happening to them.

More goodbyes. God, give me the ability to say goodbye. I didn't mind goodbyes as a four-year-old, but I've never wanted them in my life after that. I realize I'll be saying some hellos, too. Somehow, Jesus, Your look, Your interaction with me will make me know love, acceptance, celebration. How can I ever say goodbye to Ron and Chris and Dan? I can't go on and on as if things were ordinary, because I can't. Not anymore. Somehow, it is the time to be sad with others. I will look to You for that.

∽ Eighteen ∽

Dear Chris and Dan,

I do not want to write you a letter, but I have to. I want you to know that I want to be there and see you. Please know that my illness is not your fault; it is not my fault; it is not anybody's fault. Cancer like mine is uncontrollable, and the causes are unknown. It may seem "un-Christian" to be angry, but it is okay. It is okay to be angry with my illness. It takes a lot away from you both: Mom can't help as much, Dad has more stress, we have fewer fun times, we have less money, and life is not very secure. It is even okay for you to be angry with me. I disappear, I can't do as much as I like. It feels like leaving even when it isn't.

When I die, it is okay to feel very sad. It is hard for anyone to imagine ahead of time. It is both a lonely missing and a glad remembering. Your world will feel shaky sometimes, and at other times it will just feel normal. A lot of other people will feel sad, too. They will say all kinds of things, trying to be helpful, trying to deal with their own sadness. Some people may even say, "Don't cry," but that's not right. You need to cry and feel sad when you need to. Some people will say stuff about this being God's plan, and how this is all wonderful. Now it is true that God will make good out of all our lives, but He grieves, too, over the death of one of His children, and for the sorrow of those left behind. So we can hope for the goodness and desire the time when we will be together again — but we sorrow deeply over the loss now.

What is death? It is our bodies being unable to continue. In my case, the cancer will show up again and again, and finally it will try to take up all the space in my body. Then this body will stop working. The me inside my body will go to heaven — a beautiful place — where I will be able to love completely, enjoy completely, with no wrongs. But I think I will still miss you. I miss you now.

What is it like to be sick? I think it stinks. I worry about you and what will happen in your lives without me. I know my illness is very sad for me, so I know it is sad for you. Some people will say things to try and make the sadness go away when I die, but it can't go away. Anger, sadness, and disappointment are all things you can use someday to make you better men who follow Jesus.

Chris, I am so proud of you, of the young man you are becoming, of your sensitive and strong spirit, of the tender ways you have been concerned for me. Dan, I am also proud of you, for your care for me, and for how you always love to help.

I will miss the conversations that I will never have with you and with your kids. I will miss not being with my first grandchild. I will miss not being able to tell you what I think you need to know as you are growing up. Please remember my words to you as you grow:

Making decisions can't be undone. Many of my problems in life came because I didn't always make the right decisions while I was growing up. Know that you don't always make the right decisions, nobody can. Be kind to yourself. Make your choices with joy. Make decisions that you can work with throughout your life.

I love you and miss you,

Mom

To my friends:

Goodbye for a time...

This week I am not afraid. I am not suffering.

There are some things I want to tell you and some things I want to thank you for. For those of you who have cared so much, thank you. For the prayers that have been said on my behalf, thank you. Every moment of the last four years has been a pure gift. Every bit of being able to trust God in this for myself and our boys has been a gift. The underlying peace and trust in God have been a gift. Every experience of your love has been a gift.

Every time you have been encouraged by God through me has been an amazing gift. Thank you.

For the petitions of healing that have been made, and the assurances made to some that I would be healed... (there were several, and the wonder of those messages was that almost all the people who were given them were perplexed, and were careful to tell me that they "didn't usually do this sort of thing")...I want you to know that I have been healed, far beyond any comprehension that we have here. And, when you get this message, be comforted in the truth that I am home.

Speaking from this side, I know I speak only in metaphors and from my imagination, but I suspect that being home will be something like being what I have loved, but without any hindrance or lack. Somehow I think that I will be a musician, playing every instrument for the enjoyment of the Lord. I will be an artist. There will be great adventures and work that can now be accomplished. I will be able to love Christ, and I think that I will know and love you all better than ever.

Love,
Nancy

✍

Nancy Cobble went home early on Sunday morning, March 17, 1996. Her husband, Ron, was at her side.

℘ *Afterword* ℘

Nancy's memorial service was held on March 21, 1996. A tape was played of a talk Nancy had once delivered during a church service. Then Al Andrews, Nancy's counselor, shared the following:

I<small>T IS AN ODD</small> and wonderful privilege to speak about a life that has already been spoken about today. In her own words and in her own life, Nancy has been far more eloquent than I could ever be.

There are many stories about Nancy Cobble in this room today. We could start with her husband, Ron, then move to her two sons, Chris and Dan, then to her mom, good friends, in-laws, and so on. There are medical colleagues who could tell stories, patients who could tell stories, musicians at church who could tell stories. So I consider it a high honor on behalf of all of you to consolidate those stories and tell you a story that we all share together today: we all miss a very lovely woman, Nancy Cobble.

Several years ago, a very professional Dr. Cobble walked into my office and, in a manner I'm sure you'll understand if you knew Nancy, said to me, "Okay, here is my situation. Last year, I was supposed to die, and I didn't. My bags were packed for the journey home to heaven. I was ready to go, and now I have had to unpack my bags, and it feels like an odd experience. I've put my bags under the bed, but now I'm asking, 'What next?'"

She told me that she knew the cancer would probably come back, but that she had no idea when. "I don't know a lot of things right now," she told me, "but I do know before I die, I want to live. Before I die, I want to love better."

I was thinking to myself, "Remarkable, remarkable. This woman is telling me she is going to die, but in the days, months, years she has left, she wants to live better." What I didn't know at the time was I was one of several people being interviewed for the job of being her counselor — that's just how Nancy worked things. I made it through the second interview, but there was even a third interview! When I found out she'd selected me, that I'd made "the team," so to speak, I was thrilled. I was thrilled because I was prepared to say, "Woman, let me pay *you* — and you come in here and work with *me*." I knew I was sitting across from a very remarkable, courageous, godly, fun woman — and I was not about to let her go someplace else.

Over the next few years, I watched her courage as she

dipped several times back into the "valley of the shadow of death," when she entered into her other bouts with cancer. Over the next few years, I discovered what anybody who has ever helped Nancy Cobble has discovered, and that is: when you finished helping her, you found you had also been helped and given to. You found you had been nourished by her wonderful, penetrating laugh, by her kind words or even the jelly beans that she carried with her to the hospital, just so she'd have something to give the people who came to visit her.

One thing that touched me was that she made a commitment not to be mean to the people who were fighting for her life. What a different experience that must have been for some of the doctors and nurses. She also taught me about giving. She taught me that no matter the pain, we can still continue to give. She kept doing that in my presence and I was amazed. She also taught me about living. In the face of death, when many people find they want to do all the things they didn't get to do in life — like go on trips and try exotic things — Nancy said, "What I want to do is to love better and to live better. I want to love my husband, my kids, my friends, my colleagues, in new and better ways."

"I want to risk more," she told me. "I'm tired of feeling so insecure." She took counseling classes, she dabbled in art, she started writing vociferously — even publishing her first nonfiction piece in a magazine. She got involved in a women's group so she could think more about her life. She began, as she said, "to live more fully."

Nancy showed me what it means to live before you die — not just to exist, but to *live*. And as I watched her face death, she showed me what it means to die. She said, "I want to do a few things before I leave this place."

Several weeks ago, I was sitting in Nancy's living room. We were talking about this memorial service, and we all admitted that it was a very strange time to talk about her service. But Nancy had a great sense of humor about it all, and this is what she told me: "There's only one thing I don't want you to say, Al. Don't tell everyone I'm having a great old time up in heaven when you are at my funeral because somehow, that doesn't fit me. I know I'll be in heaven, and I know it will be wonderful, but the idea of me frolicking around having a great time while you are all crying just doesn't work for me."

I thought to myself, "Well, that's Nancy." So then I asked her, "Well, what does work?" We talked for a while before she said, "Remember that verse in John? The one about not letting your hearts be troubled, that in my Father's house are many rooms — and that I go to prepare a place for you?" I said yes, and after we talked for a while, the image that came to us was that Nancy would be preparing a place for all of us, that there was a table being set in heaven, and that she was a woman, a wife, a daughter, a mother, who was preparing a place with Christ, setting the table for those who would one day come to dinner. We came to the conclusion that she would be waiting for us, and that one day, hopefully, we'd all show up.

So, Nancy, there it is: I didn't say you were happy, but I told everyone you are preparing a place.

There is a passage in Hebrews that talks about the people of faith, the people who have gone before us: Abraham, Moses, Isaac, the people who believed in what they could not see, and lived as if it were going to happen. Abraham was promised a land, and he lived as if he were going to live in that land — even though he never got to.

If there was any way I could do it, I'd like to add my friend Nancy to that list. She was a woman who lived by faith, a woman who lived in the now as if she could see beyond — and did things as if she could, too.

At the end of that passage it talks about all the people of faith, and it tells us, as we look at them, we should respond like this: as you look at Abraham, Isaac, Jacob and those who have gone before; as you look at our dear friend, Nancy, who had faith during such dark, dark, days, and since we are surrounded by such a great cloud of witnesses, let us throw off everything that hinders and the sin that so easily entangles, and let us run with perseverance the race set before us. Let's fix our eyes on Jesus, the author and perfecter of our faith, who for the joy set before Him endured the cross, despising the shame, and sat down at the right hand of the throne of the Father.

I believe that as we remember the saints of old, as we remember our dear friend, and as we remember stories we could tell for hours, the greatest honor we could give

Nancy and her family this day is to be people committed to living before we die, people who struggle to know the God who is trustworthy, and to be people who eagerly, eagerly await a feast at a table that I believe Nancy is helping to set, even now.

THE WOMAN WITH WINGS
(FOR NANCY COBBLE)

yes, friend,
we all watched you
        grow wings.

oh, not white-
gauzy-billowing
too-good-to-be-true
wings of wonder,

as if your pilgrimage
were the journey of cherubs,
and not men.

no, sweet angel,

your halo was hope —
&
you wore it proudly

like a blazing auburn crown,
like a shining red jewel,
like a bright, beautiful
beacon of truth,

flooding our lives
with the brilliant ache
you felt

from holding both heaven
& earth,
all in one handful.

"what do you do,"
we once asked,

"what do you do
when your heart shatters
like stained glass
as you learn to tell
your family goodbye?"

"oh," you said, "we cry."

"then we carve pumpkins
at halloween;

we giggle

& have sword fights
with string cheese."

yes, friend of ours:
you *were* given wings.

in the midst of your weariness,
we watched
your heart mount up
like an eagle.

& like you,
dear friend,

we learned
we could
both weep & laugh

that bright
& sorrowful
morning

when our Son of
Righteousness
arose
& came for you
at last

healing in His

wings

JOY SAWYER